The Activity Book That Will Transform Your Life

Featuring 55 Adult Activities: Coloring, Sudoku, Dot-to-Dot, Word Searches, Mazes, Fallen Phrases, Math Logic, Word Tiles, Color by Number, Spot the Difference, Draw the Other Half, Nanograms, Brick-by-Brick, Word Scramble, and Much More!

Tamara L Adams

Each page has a fun adult activity.

Thank you for your purchase!
I hope you enjoy this book that is dedicated to
all of you who love to travel!!

Please consider leaving a review and checking out my
Amazon collection!

Contact me to get a free printable PDF of activities at:
http://www.tamaraladamsauthor.com/free-printable-activity-book-pdf/

http://www.amazon.com/T.L.-Adams/e/B00YSROGC4

tamaraadamsauthor@gmail.com

www.tamaraladamsauthor.com

https://twitter.com/@TamaraLAdams

https://www.facebook.com/TamaraLAdamsAuthor/

https://www.pinterest.com/tamara-l-adams-author/

All Cartoon Drawings are from https://publicdomainvectors.org

Solve the Maze: Start in the opening at the top and work your way to the opening at the bottom.

Answer on page 56

Spot the 9 differences between the images

Answer on page 56

Search for the baseball related words

Assist	Bases	Loaded
Batter	Fielder	DoubleHeader
Gear	Helmet	KnuckleBall
Lineup	PinchHitter	Run
Outfield	Steal	Strike
Throw	Umpire	
Walk	Mound	

Answer on page 56

```
                                        I   X
R  R  E  D  A  E  H  E  L  B  U  O  D  V  B  C  M     F  M
E  F  H  L  M  P  A  S  S  I  S  T  U  E  D  S  E     I  C
T  I                                      Z  V        A  E
T  H     T  E  M  L  E  H  S  J  M  N  S     G  D     U  F
I  R     D  Y  Z  C  Y  V  D  B  L  K  E     H  L     A  O
H  U     N  L                 B  Y     O  E        S  P
H  N     U  I     F  T  N  Y  S     S  A     Z  I     A  F
C  W     O  N     S  T  E  A  L     T  W     B  F     Q  J
N  I     M  E     P  H     P  Y     R  W     D  T     P  D
I  T     H  U     P  G     X  K     I  L     J  U     Z  Z
P  F     O  P     C  Y           K  B     F  O     R  R
Q  R     R  F     D  K  L  A  W  X  E  D     R  N     F  B
B  A     J  H     P  Z  D  X  S  F  S  Q     L  F     L  Y
E  E     L  Q                          Q  J     M  Z
R  G     L  Z  K  N  U  C  K  L  E  B  A  L  L  R     F  T
I  N     L  A  G  R  X  W  D  E  D  A  O  L  T  G     I  A
P  G                                      L  L
M  F  I  E  L  D  E  R  L  T  R  L  X  P  O  B  A  S  E  S
U  P  E  F  Z  D  N  B  A  T  T  E  R  C  N  W  O  R  H  T
```

Connect the dots from 100 to 205.
Don't let the extra numbers fool you!

Answer on page 56

258
218
268
240
151   152   233   233   264   244
157   257
223   246   248   163   245
238   150   153   162   164   252   242   238
243   161   247   249   165   237   237
140   149   154   253   250   166
139   141   254   160   255   249   167   272   184   236
148   254   255   246   168
142   155   247
138   265   251   159   169
270   143   147   253   156   158   254   183   213
271   137   244   157   245   170   238   279
144   146   252   229   185
256   230   242   145   251   171   236   182   278
262   136   276   250   223   172   220   275
268   241   212   173   243   181   272   186   211
135   269   239   180   187
240   179
134   241   214   210   174   248   257   178   188
259   239   133   274   194   175   189
237   132   238   262   176   177   190   265
239   193   259   191
236   131   237   222   195   192   264   266
130   236   259   226   261   258   268   245   260
225   196   256   271   263   263
235   129   211   239   277   236   239   250
279   126   197
128   127   212   275   267
217   266   210   198
125   238   249
214   207   209
226   248
124   215   213   271   278   261   243   236
230   231   199
123   274   260   241   269
228   235   265   276   273
122   276   206   200   239   237
260   222   217   269
234   121   264   215   275
263   120   278   256   218   273   267
277   216   231   209   272   201
270   220   261   266   274   246
119   227   247   208
262   279   237   270   229   224
118   253   238   228   202
251   242   225
234   117   224   252   244   273   203
116   240   227   204
258   115   257   216   255
267   114   105   104   103   102   101   100   205
111   106
113   112   110   109
108   107

4

These are the rules of Sudoku Answer on page 56

Numbers from 1 to 9 are inserted into sets that have 9 x 9 = 81 squares in whole. Every number can be used just once in every, 3x3 block, column and row.

- Every number can be used just once in the blocks of 3 x 3 = 9 square blocks.
- Each row of 9 numbers ought to contain all digits 1 through 9 in any order
- Every column of 9 numbers should comprise all digits 1 through 9 in any order

One way to figure out which numbers can go in each space is to use "process of elimination" by checking to see which other numbers are already included within each square – since there can be no duplication of numbers 1-9 within each square (or row or column).

2			3	7		6	1	
6			8	2	1	3	4	
	3	9				2	7	8
3	9		5	1	8		2	4
5	2	4	7	3	6	8	9	
8	1	7		4	2	5		
9	5				7	1	3	6
4	8	1	2	6	3		5	7
7		3	1	9		4	8	

Draw the image to it's corresponding square

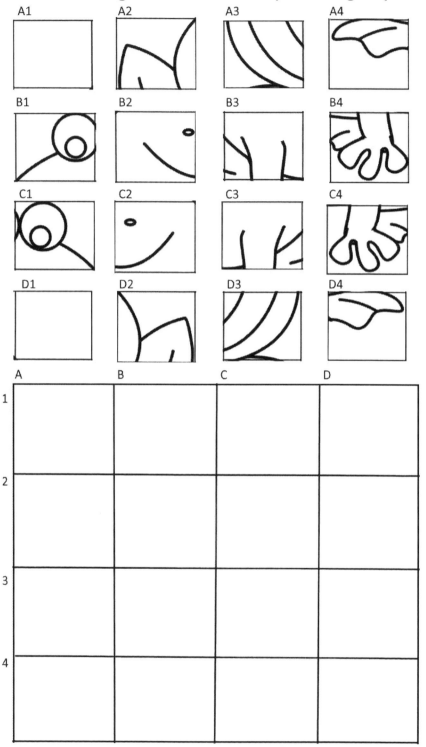

Image on page 56

Unscramble each of the Reptile words. Take the letters that appear in ◯ boxes and unscramble them for the final message.

Answer on page 56

GILTOALAR

KAISISBL

BDDAERE NOGRAD

CEENMHOAL

CONR NESKA

RICCLODOE

GLSAS ZILRAD

GIAAUN

KODOOM NADGOR

RIOMONT LISZARD

NTEAIDP TELUTR

TERKSNAELAT

ESA TURLET

GIPPNNAS RELTUT

TIOTOSRE

TAWRE NOCSIACM

Quest Rules

Answer on page 57

Your task is to fill every empty cell with a positive or negative integer in such a way so that each white cell's value equals the sum of its adjoining half-height cells. When complete, each Balance Quest puzzle grid will "balance" itself in such a way so that the four center cells surrouding the center "zero cell" will always add up to zero.

There are five rules that must be followed in every Quest puzzle:
The grey cells must include all integers between -16 and 16, except 0
No number can be repeated within any of the grey cells.
No number can be repeated within any of the white cells.
The number in each white cell must equal the sum of its adjoining cells.
The center Zero cell is always the sum of all four adjacent cells.

** Numbers can (and will) be reused across both white and grey cells. The rules specify only that numbers can never be used more than once in cells of the same color.

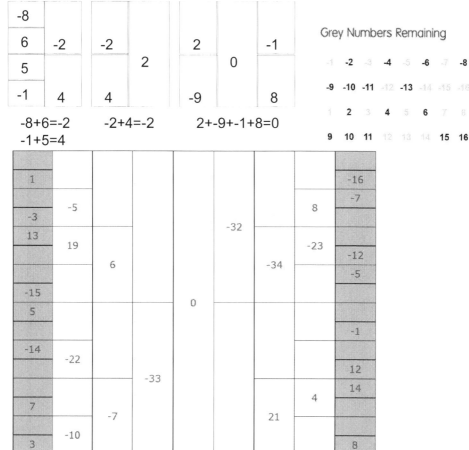

	-8						
6	-2	-2		2		-1	
5			2		0		
-1	4	4		-9		8	

-8+6=-2   -2+4=-2   2+-9+-1+8=0
-1+5=4

Grey Numbers Remaining

-1 **-2** -3 **-4** -5 **-6** -7 **-8**

-9 **-10** **-11** -12 **-13** -14 -15 -16

1 **2** 3 **4** 5 **6** 7 8

9 **10** **11** 12 13 14 **15** **16**

Answer on page 57

Find the 10 ✔ check marks in image
Then have fun coloring!

Solve the Maze: Start in the opening at the top and work your way to the opening in the center of the circle.

Answer on page 57

Letter Tiles

Answer on page 57

Move the tiles around to make the
correct phrase.
The three letters on each tile must
stay together and in the given order.

E L I	S O N	R E A	S I	G E T	D B	L .	T W
O R K	R E A	N E	H E	E O	L T	A L	I T
A N	A T	E V E	W I L	T H	S O N	T W	O N '
T H	F O R						

Find the 1 image that is different from the rest

Answer on page 57

The rules of the cryptogram puzzle:

You are given a piece of text where each letter is substituted with a number and you need to work out which letter in the native alphabet is being coded by the numbers you are given.

You need to use logic and knowledge of the letters and words of the language to crack the cipher and work out the message by working out which number is representing each letter.

Answer on page 57

Hint: One of the words is *Direction*

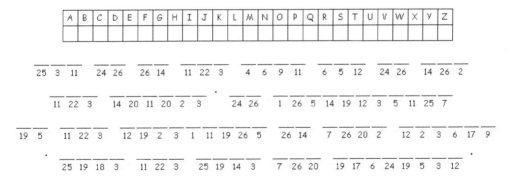

A	B	C	D	E	F	G	H	I	J	K	L	M	N	O	P	Q	R	S	T	U	V	W	X	Y	Z

25 3 11   24 26   26 14   11 22 3   4 6 9 11   6 5 12   24 26   14 26 2

11 22 3   14 20 11 20 2 3   24 26   1 26 5 14 19 12 3 5 11 25 7

19 5   11 22 3   12 19 2 3 1 11 19 26 5   26 14   7 26 20 2   12 2 3 6 17 9

25 19 18 3   11 22 3   25 19 14 3   7 26 20   19 17 6 24 19 5 3 12

The goal of this puzzle is to figure out how to fit the numbered bricks into the square of bricks without changing their shape or breaking them into smaller pieces.

Answer on page 57

Unscramble each of the Tree words. Take the letters that appear in ☐ boxes and unscramble them for the final message.

Answer on page 57

LEPPA

SENPA

LAKBC SAH

RCBIH

HUNTTCES

TOTNOOCODW

LAGDOSU RFI

PASTUCLEYU

EEGERRVNE

FGI

KIONGG

KEOLCHM

KIHYORC

RENJIUP

TUKQUAM

CTLUOS

LGAOMAIN

MAGYANOH

NETEARNCI

KOA

PEPRA RCBIH

WODREDO

IOQUASE

YCESOMRA

GEPNIWE LOWLWI

Have Fun Coloring!

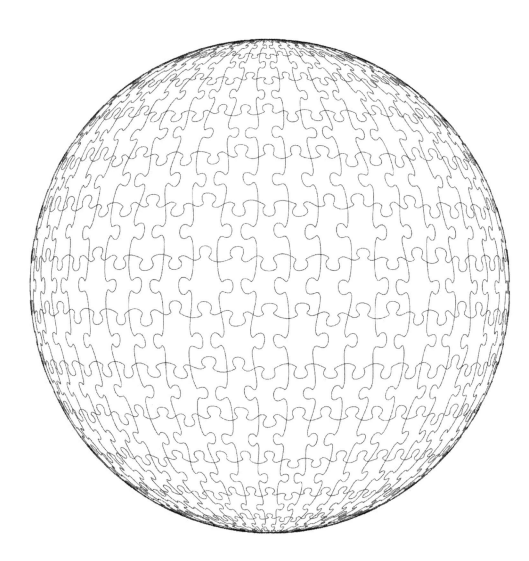

Numbers from 1 to 9 are inserted into sets that have 9 x 9 = 81 squares in whole. Every number can be used just once in every, 3x3 block, column and row.

- Every number can be used just once in the blocks of 3 x 3 = 9 square blocks.
- Each row of 9 numbers ought to contain all digits 1 through 9 in any order
- Every column of 9 numbers should comprise all digits 1 through 9 in any order

One way to figure out which numbers can go in each space is to use "process of elimination" by checking to see which other numbers are already included within each square – since there can be no duplication of numbers 1-9 within each square (or row or column).

	1	6						
	8	9	5	1				
	7			9				6
	6			8		3	2	7
7		2			1	8		
9		8	2	3	7	1		5
	9							3
3	5		9		8		7	1
8			7			6		9

The goal consists in finding the black boxes in each grid.

The figures given on the side and in top of the grid indicate the numbers of black boxes in the line or the column on which they are.

For example 3,3 on the left of a line indicates that there is, from left to right, a block of 3 black boxes then a block of 3 black boxes on this line.
To solve a puzzle, one needs to determine which cells will be boxes and which will be empty. Determining which cells are to be left empty (called spaces) is as important as determining which to fill (called boxes). Later in the solving process, the spaces help determine where a clue (continuing block of boxes and a number in the legend) may spread. Solvers usually use a dot or a cross to mark cells they are certain are spaces.

It is also important never to guess. Only cells that can be determined by logic should be filled. An example is shown here.

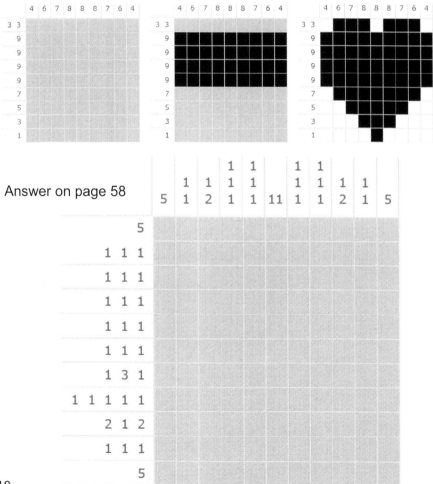

Answer on page 58

Number Blocks

Answer on page 58

Try to fill in the missing numbers.

The missing numbers are integers between 1 and 9.
The numbers in each row add up to totals to the right.
The numbers in each column add up to the totals along
the bottom. Numbers can be repeated.
The diagonal lines also add up the totals to the right.

				14
	4			18
			7	20
8		1		23
	6		7	19
24	23	13	20	21

Connect the dots from 100 to 167
Don't let the extra numbers fool you!

Answer on page 58

191
274   284
239   277   265   126   263   127   275   258
236   276 273   125   128
         276 273   272   266   254   248   253
            123 124   271 262   261   129
176   122   264   260 269   270   192
   254   121   258   257   267   130
238   120   251 131
         292   279
   255   245   119   249   268 256   259   133   132
              288   281   134
251   237   299   298   168
250   242   118   180   139 264 135 173   242
         287   265   259
247 293 238   297   296   140 263   138   286   273
                                    100 141 266   136   172 268
244   295   167 142 261   257   174   271
      117 234   262 255   166   137   169   274 275 171
236   235   217   294 101   260 143   144   175
                              289   267 208 207 256 269   145
   231   102   276   270
236   301   300   214   216   206 193 177 146   170
   238 116 103   218 219   277 178   278
230   249   246   164 220   155   154 151 179 147
         248   215   279 302   156   221   153 152   150 148 280
252   222 243 205   226   149
                   253   157   223   181
241   224 115 104 210 213   229 228 272   204   190   282   250
   114   240 239 105 211   163 158   194   203 195 189 182
225   237 237 106 162   232 202 196 188 183   283
113 238   212 161   160   303   201 197   186 185   184   247
   111   110 109 107   159   200 198   252
      239 209   291   290   285   243
112   236   108   245   241   199
         244   240 239   246
                                         237
```

21
```

The goal of this puzzle is to figure out how to fit the numbered bricks into the triangle of bricks without changing their shape or breaking them into smaller pieces. Answer on page 58

20

Fallen Phrases

Answer on page 58

A fallen phrase puzzle is a puzzle where all the letters have fallen to the bottom. They got mixed up on their way down, but remain in the same row. You complete the puzzle by filling the letters into the column they fall under. You start by filling in the one-letter columns, because those clearly don't have anywhere else to go in their column.

Also try filling in common one-, two- and three-letter words as shown in the example below.

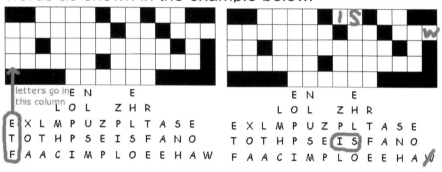

Draw the other half, then color or
Add your own touches to the image.

Answer on page 58

Find the 11 ⅄ in the image then color it!

Solve the Maze: start at the top and work to the bottom

Answer on page 59

Math Squares

Answer on page 59

Try to fill in the missing numbers.

Use the numbers 1 through 9 to complete the equations.

Each number is only used once.
Each row is a math equation.
Work from left to right.
Each column is a math equation.
Work from top to bottom.

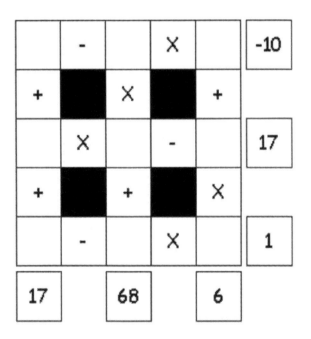

Have Fun Coloring!

Search for the words

Answer on page 59

Animals	Backpack	Campfire
Fishing	Equipment	Campground
Hike	Hammock	Flashlight
Insect	Map	Path
Bag	Tent	Sleeping
Wildlife	Lake	

```
                        O  L  D
                  B  K  Y  G  A  B  N  C  L
               K  K  G  O  X  C  S  T  M  U  X  G  R
            M  T  W  A  F  L  A  S  H  L  I  G  H  T  F  V  P
         P  B  N  L  E  O  M  S  H  E  X  U  T  F  T  J  V  M  R
      U  F  V  E  N  C  P  H  X  Z  J  Y  U  I  D  U  E  S  N  Q  K
      P  S  Q  T  K  G  A  R  G  S  F  K  S  F  V  R  L  N  I  C  C
   Y  X  S  R  E  R              M  N  L  H  K           G  M  J  M  L  R
   Y  D  S  D  O  F              P  M  I  A  X           E  O  V  F  C  G
U  Z  A  W  U  F  B  I  Q  X  V  N  U  X  M  E  R  I  F  P  M  A  C  L  J
A  G  U  N  F  B  A  Y  L  H  G  Q  J  Q  Q  I  O  A  K  H  I  K  E  X  E
R  Z  D  D  Y  I  C  Z  D  D  D  J  S  T  O  W  N  U  B  E  U  J  C  K  J
I  V  D  N  G  C  D  K  K  P  Z  L  K  L  J  S  C  D  A  T  J  D  I  B  O  X  L
L  U  P  E  T  N  W  P  L  Z  U  Z  I  P  Y  A  O  Q  Q  K  S  A  S  O  S  F  Z
P  J  J  D  F  S  R  A  H  V  Z  Y  L  W  F  E  Q  U  I  P  M  E  N  T  K  K  J
F  W  I  C     A  C  C  Q  L  C  J  A  B  O  Z  G  N  P  U        M  I  C  D
N  V  H  Z        K  C  O  M  M  A  H  B  Z  N  X  R  O           P  B  S  A
K  F  Y  W  E        V  N  W  V  A  D  H  R  Z  I  H           Q  L  S  M  U
   N  D  B  Q  O                                            S  I  U  C  G
   H  C  J  H  V  F                                       N  Y  X  E  L  W
      R  L  O  F  R  V  T  C  E  S  N  I  P  H  T  A  P  X  H  C  X
      T  I  P  S  T  X  S  L  E  E  P  I  N  G  U  U  J  V  R  F  C
         A  O  D  T  R  J  Y  B  M  D  W  S  B  X  I  G  X  W  Y
            M  N  D  N  Z  L  E  K  A  L  U  Y  O  D  Q  G  E
               I  X  Y  V  O  W  N  P  S  K  B  Z  M
                  W  P  I  Q  M  S  T  R  D
                     X  N  L
```

Letter Tiles

Answer on page 59

Move the tiles around to make the correct phrase.
The three letters on each tile must stay together and in the given order.

E R S	T O D	S S I	O N	O O D	T Y	T E	T H
M .	O N	S E E	M A K	E I	A Y	O U R	A N D
E G	T O	T H E	M I	L L	O N	E P	I N

29

Find the 1 image that is different from the rest

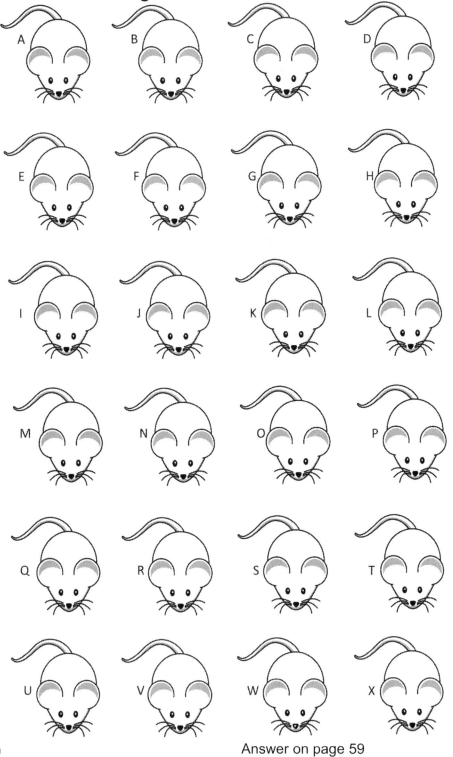

Answer on page 59

The goal of this puzzle is to figure out how to fit the numbered bricks into the rectangle of bricks without changing their shape or breaking them into smaller pieces.   Answer on page 59

| 4 | 4 | 4 |

| 11 |

| 12 | 12 |
| 12 | 12 |

| 3 | 3 |
| 3 | 3 | 3 |

| 7 |
| 7 |
| 7 | 7 | 7 |

| 12 |
| 12 |

6	6	6
	6	6
6	6	6

| 10 |
| 10 | 10 |
| 10 | 10 | 10 |

| 9 |
| 9 |
| 9 |
| 9 |
| 9 | 9 | 9 | 9 |

| 2 |
| 2 | 2 |
| 2 |

| 5 | 5 | 5 |
| 5 | 5 | 5 | 5 |

| 1 | 1 | 1 | 1 | 1 |

| 8 | 8 | 8 | 8 |
| 8 | 8 | 8 | 8 |

These are the rules of sudoku
Answer on page 59

Numbers from 1 to 9 are inserted into sets that have 9 x 9 = 81 squares in whole. Every number can be used just once in every, 3x3 block, column and row.

- Every number can be used just once in the blocks of 3 x 3 = 9 square blocks.
- Each row of 9 numbers ought to contain all digits 1 through 9 in any order
- Every column of 9 numbers should comprise all digits 1 through 9 in any order

One way to figure out which numbers can go in each space is to use "process of elimination" by checking to see which other numbers are already included within each square – since there can be no duplication of numbers 1-9 within each square (or row or column).

4		7	9		5		8	2
6	5	1	3		2		7	
	8	9	4	1		6		
7			2	5		3	6	1
9	6			7	8	2	4	5
1			6	3	4		9	
8	1	2	7			5		
		6						7
			8		3	9	1	6

Answer on page 60

Solve the Maze: Start in the opening
at the top and work your way to the
opening in the center of the triangle.

How starfish can you find?

Answer on page 60

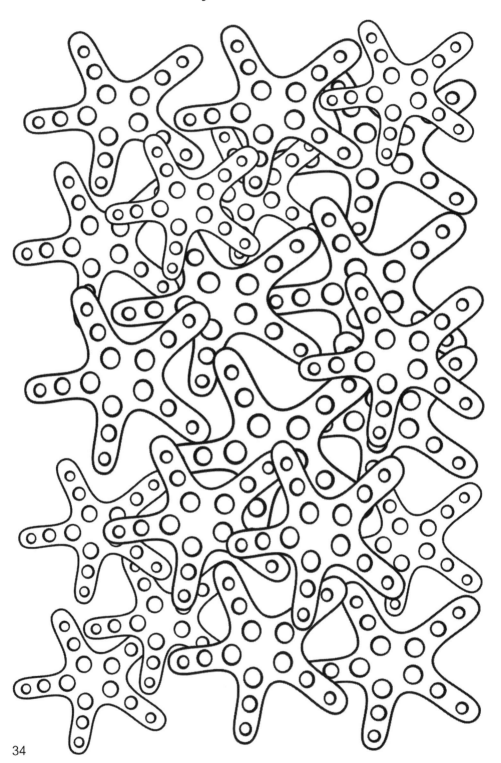

Color by Number

1=Light Blue   4=Black/Grey

2=Dark Blue   3=Green

Find the 1 image that is different from the rest
Answer on page 60

Search for the words

Artist	Carve	Chalk	Clay
Draw	Easel	Film	Glaze
Graffiti	Hue	Ink	Media
Model	Palette	Pen	Paint
Quill	Sketch	Varnish	Watercolor

```
R N T R V        L Y F O Y        P S P S A        T O B S V
F I N F D        M T R P A        A B T P W        S E Z Y A
S M W R G        M W V E F        R A O O D        B F X O L
S I V C Y        Y O C B L        K Z H B T        J Y E H J
A X F D Q        Y Z W M T        E U Q H T        Q K U P J

        C S H S C        Z L S B T        C W L D R        Y O K S G
        P U V Z Y        I X I D T        Y A C L A        A B L Q A
        E D V D V        A S V F E        X G T J Q        W V T M K
        G K U I H        O U K D P        U J X R H        M N A Y O
        U I Z V Q        G D Z R K        S I L E A        I R H Q M

B V W N B        L V O B V        O I M B U        X E L T A
W Y A U R        F E N S K        S C M C W        G H R P P
N G R L T        T N S P G        L I F F S        M I F J V
S Q D P J        O R Y A O        L M T U H        B M G N H
I H I K A        U I M X E        P R X M P        V N Y Y M

        L M R U N        C V N T Y        D U B C P        C G D A A
        Z M I Z L        D L R O V        S N P F Z        K E V R L
        V T W M F        O C A J K        X F I Y W        B I T Q P
        P H T T K        L O K Y O        T G C G H        U I N L A
        T W L Q N        F D Y V V        H P W I F        S Q U K T

V Z X C W        J B R H A        O W T R C        Y L G O T
N A S E J        C H A L K        H J J T K        C S C L R
M O R A V        I K V V V        O V E L V        J A E L P
W L W N U        X A Z Y Z        G K S D I        Q D V B Q
Q C N Y I        D M B T A        S L Y B V        O L D I S

        S T A K B        A L U Z H        Q D V N M        Z D Y Y I
        A H Y E N        Y I A Y D        C A R V E        R A H U N
        C L Z C B        L D D G I        U W U N K        P U O G N
        Z A W E A        W W U E A        S I K I M        N I Q S U
        L P N R R        L U V E M        T H V X H        N E G T B

P L Q S G        O P U A U        R B J E I        A B E G E
I F U J G        B L X C R        N Y W F P        S B U P N
S I I M M        P E O O D        M R F O E        Q F A J O
H L L J F        P A M C X        D A F G R        E E M F Y
D M L T L        X P W U R        R Z K V M        T S V L H

        U N J M Q        E N X V G        T H V B T        C P V B L
        B P A L M        A T I T O        T F D E J        R W A X B
        B J Z N C        J X A T Q        C E L O M        S D V E P
        W K U A O        V H F W P        X A C N M        N L U E Z
        T P O E I        B A F E V        P E S T H        G A J W M
```

37

Draw the other half, then color or
Add your own touches to the image.

Connect the dots from 100 to 153
Don't let the extra numbers fool you!

Answer on page 60

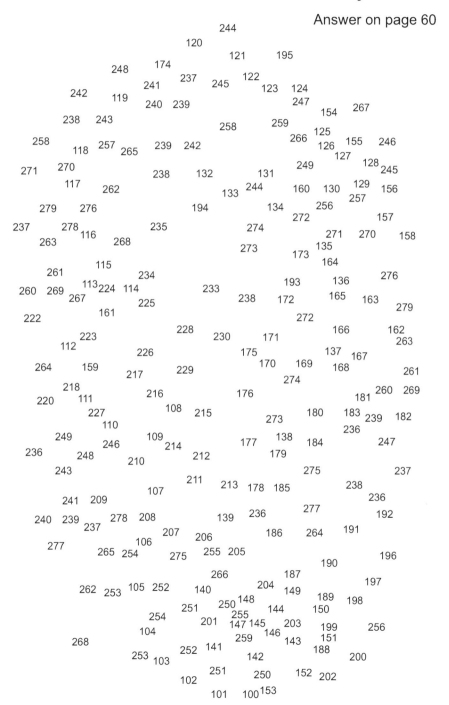

Unscramble each of the Kind words. Take the letters that appear in boxes and unscramble them for the final message.

Answer on page 60

CEAPACCENT

AITFNCEFO

LISBS

NACSOPSOIM

DITLEGHDE

NAMDEORE

TAFCISNEDA

REESOUGN

TIDFAETAUN

BIONIJTLUA

MISTIMPO

LEFCEUAP

RAUPETR

REENYIST

TALQIURN

Solve the Maze: Start in the opening at the top and work your way to the opening in the middle.

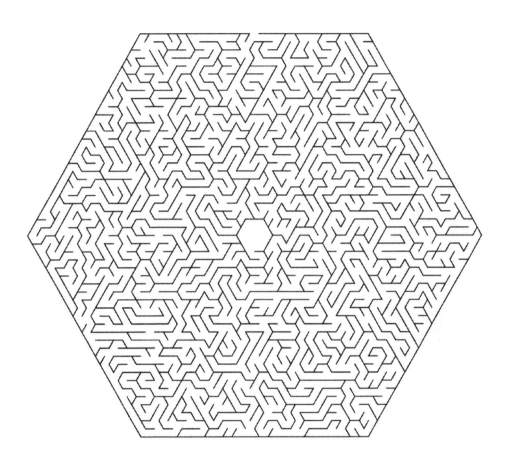

The goal consists in finding the black boxes in each grid.

The figures given on the side and in top of the grid indicate the numbers of black boxes in the line or the column on which they are.

For example 3,3 on the left of a line indicates that there is, from left to right, a block of 3 black boxes then a block of 3 black boxes on this line.
To solve a puzzle, one needs to determine which cells will be boxes and which will be empty. Determining which cells are to be left empty (called spaces) is as important as determining which to fill (called boxes). Later in the solving process, the spaces help determine where a clue (continuing block of boxes and a number in the legend) may spread. Solvers usually use a dot or a cross to mark cells they are certain are spaces.

It is also important never to guess. Only cells that can be determined by logic should be filled. An example is shown here.

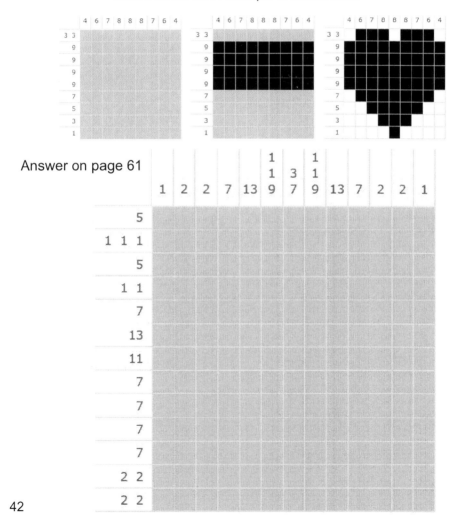

Answer on page 61

Draw the image to it's corresponding square

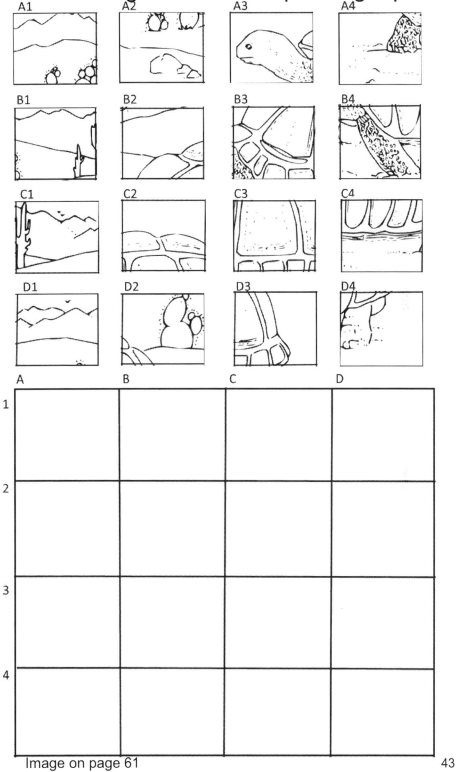

Number Blocks

Answer on page 61

Try to fill in the missing numbers.

The missing numbers are integers between 1 and 9.
The numbers in each row add up to totals to the right.
The numbers in each column add up to the totals along
the bottom. Numbers can be repeated.
The diagonal lines also add up the totals to the right.

				20
		3	9	18
	9	1		25
3				14
		5		17
20	18	13	23	16

Spot the 10 differences between the images

Answer on page 61

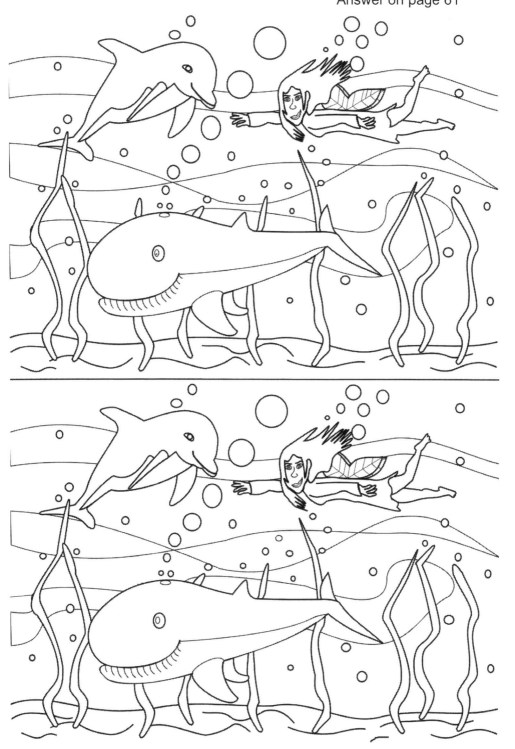

45

Have Fun Coloring!

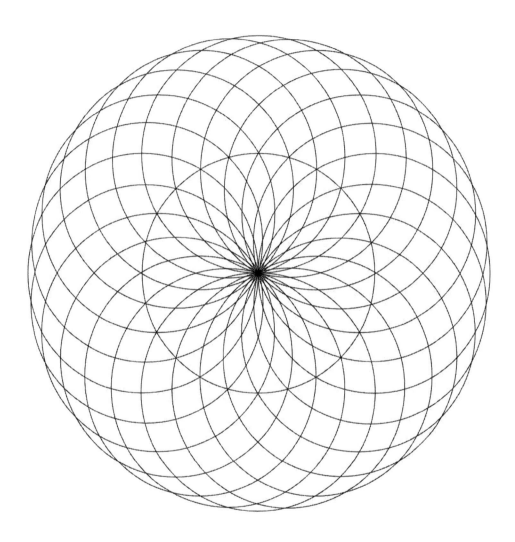

Letter Tiles

Answer on page 61

Move the tiles around to make the correct phrase.
The three letters on each tile must stay together and in the given order.

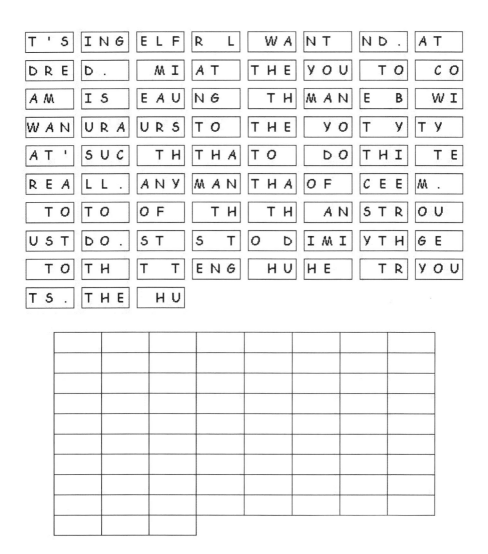

T ' S	I N G	E L F	R L	W A	N T	N D .	A T
D R E	D .	M I	A T	T H E	Y O U	T O	C O
A M	I S	E A U	N G	T H	M A N	E B	W I
W A N	U R A	U R S	T O	T H E	Y O	T Y	T Y
A T '	S U C	T H	T H A	T O	D O	T H I	T E
R E A	L L .	A N Y	M A N	T H A	O F	C E E	M .
T O	T O	O F	T H	T H	A N	S T R	O U
U S T	D O .	S T	S T	O D	I M I	Y T H	G E
T O	T H	T T	E N G	H U	H E	T R	Y O U
T S .	T H E	H U					

Search for the words

Answer on page 61

Argentina Australia Bangladesh Brazil Canada
Cambodia Denmark Guatemala Haiti Japan
Ecuador Estonia Kazakhstan India Greece
Iceland Morocco Luxembourg Syria Romania
Venezuela Ukraine Madagascar Yemen Sweden
Zimbabwe Turkey Netherlands France Nicaragua

```
Y A A I N L Y T E Q N T E R C T R J A G B N P X A
D N K C B U Z C X O T V Q Z T E I B D F B H I Y X
O L I E D R E F N O M D M B R S U T H N M J C Q G
J R Z E L E M I T E J L E C D T X T L Q W Z E N F
Z P J C R P C W W O I M J Z L O T I X H M M L R K
J G Z G A A D F O S B T G T T N O L B M L V A H P
D V X H R R C H F G Y D V D A I C G C K N N N A V
O C A A Z N B J I E E R E P C A V U M Y C B D R W
X W G I Z O W M A C F E I O G C K L M E D Q K Q A
K U K T I X R D P E Z Q J A H Y E U R G Z X O V R
A R E I B J C Z G A H I X A R Q U W F S Z U F I O
S L N C P Q S Y F L D A Z V H E M T X U V R R K K
K P G J V W G D M M Z R E Q B W W M M O O P Q D D
C P H I B A D A N A C C A U K C G B D V F R I V D
H P W M G M W W P A Y M L Q M S G U A T E M A L A
K V U S H T Q O P L L A V O S B T K J B D J N W I
K R A M N E D R U H U R R R F Z R R N C M U E Y D
R R Z I K O L Z J I R O E Y M Y D A B F I I R H O
A R F W N Z H R X W C P E H U Y N I Z Z U Z Z M B
O I E R N A P A I C R M J F T E G N H I I D N Q M
U V D L C C T C O O E B C A G E E E V H L Z K L A
O L I N N N C S D N Q K X W S A N Y N Y G W C D C
R V Y J I I C A H H I F X Y H P W W G L C X E N N
F P G Y Y N U G F K Y V P Q B W N N M M R G T G F
F S T S K C M A Z U A R G E N T I N A C V M N R E
R N A T E F G D G Y M Z V E M D H K W J I X T T S
V I R K B R K A W L Y E A M Z F H O N K T B Y L H
S L G J V Y C M G F N X B K N E D E W S W C G C U
G X A Y G X Q K D E Q A S W J T W C X W B E F A F
Y K I B L N T D Z S X C N B R A A I L A R T S U A
E Z N Y V V Z J U Q I Q N Y X Z I P M Q F A U F C L
K Z A D F P E H S E D A L G N A B A D J B C Z P Q
R P M X J L S N Y T W D H K L R F D N P S E P F D
U M O Y A K M P J F U D D Z D E L B U C U G R K A
T A R J E B P G R U O B M E X U L G U V S A U Q Y
```

Find the 1 image that is different from the rest

Answer on page 61

49

Fallen Phrases

Answer on page 62

A fallen phrase puzzle is a puzzle where all the letters have fallen to the bottom. They got mixed up on their way down, but remain in the same row.

You complete the puzzle by filling the letters into the column they fall under. You start by filling in the one-letter columns, because those clearly don't have anywhere else to go in their column as shown in the example below.

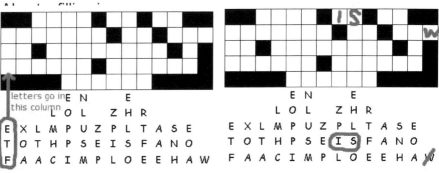

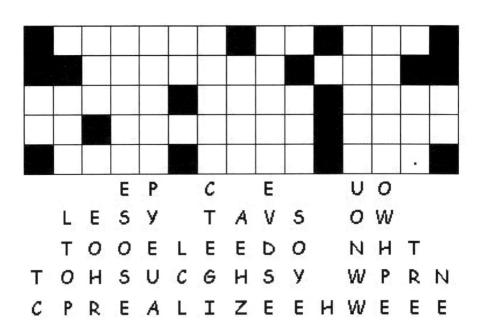

Math Squares

Answer on page 62

Try to fill in the missing numbers.

Use the numbers 1 through 9 to complete the equations.

Each number is only used once.
Each row is a math equation.
Work from left to right.
Each column is a math equation.
Work from top to bottom.

	+		+		17
×	■	×	■	-	
	×		+		12
+	■	-	■	-	
	×		-		38
29		1		-7	

Answer on page 62

Solve the Maze: Start in the opening at the top and work your way to the opening in the middle.

Quest Rules

Answer on page 62

Your task is to fill every empty cell with a positive or negative integer in such a way so that each white cell's value equals the sum of its adjoining half-height cells. When complete, each Balance Quest puzzle grid will "balance" itself in such a way so that the four center cells surrouding the center "zero cell" will always add up to zero.

There are five rules that must be followed in every Quest puzzle:
The grey cells must include all integers between -16 and 16, except 0
No number can be repeated within any of the grey cells.
No number can be repeated within any of the white cells.
The number in each white cell must equal the sum of its adjoining cells.
The center Zero cell is always the sum of all four adjacent cells.

** Numbers can (and will) be reused across both white and grey cells. The rules specify only that numbers can never be used more than once in cells of the same color.

-8

6	-2	-2		2		-1
5			2		0	
-1	4	4		-9		8

-8+6=-2   -2+4=-2   2+-9+-1+8=0
-1+5=4

Grey Numbers Remaining

-1 **-2 -3** -4 **-5 -6** -7 -8
-9 -10 -11 **-12 -13 -14** -15 -16
1 2 **3 4** 5 6 7 8
9 10 11 12 **13** 14 **15 16**

Medium

5								12
-1	15						2	-8
		22						
7	10					-14		-15
-7		-2						
			0					2
6						-24		-11
				-28				
-10								8
			-53					-4
11	20					-6		
		49						
14								-16

53

Letter Tiles

Answer on page 62

Move the tiles around to make the correct phrase.
The three letters on each tile must stay together and in the given order.

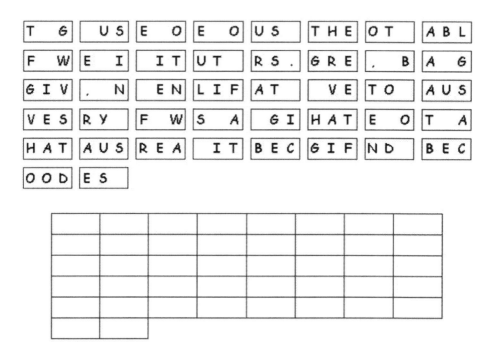

The goal of this puzzle is to figure out how to fit the numbered bricks into the square of bricks without changing their shape or breaking them into smaller pieces.

Answer on page 62

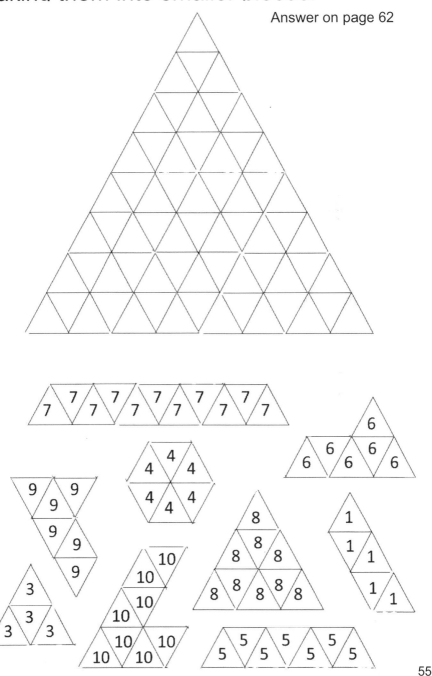

Page 1

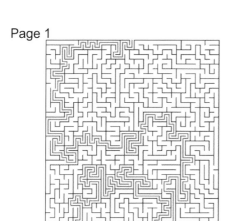

Page 2

Page 3

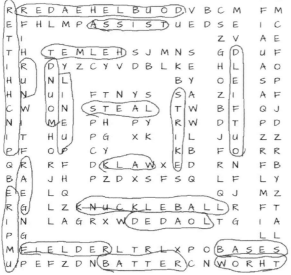

Page 4

Page 5

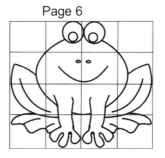

Page 6

Page 7

Alligator
Basilisk
Bearded Dragon
Chameleon
Corn Snake
Crocodile
Glass lizard
Iguana
Komodo Dragon
Monitor Lizards
Painted Turtle
Rattlesnake
Sea Turtle
Snapping Turtle
Tortoise
Water moccasin

Gecko

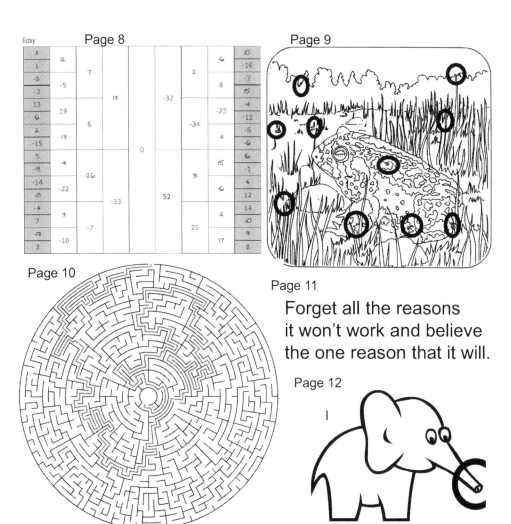

Page 8

Easy

(number grid solution)

Page 9

Page 10

Page 11

Forget all the reasons
it won't work and believe
the one reason that it will.

Page 12

Let go of the past and go for the future. Go confidently in
the direction of your Dreams. Live the life you imagined.

Page 14

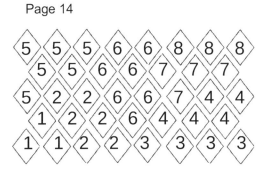

Page 15

Apple	Juniper
Aspen	Kumquat
Black Ash	Locust
Birch	Magnolia
Chestnut	Mahogany
Cottonwood	Nectarine
Douglas Fir	Oak
Eucalyptus	Paper Birch
Evergreen	Redwood
Fig	Sequoia
Gingko	Sycamore
Hemlock	Weeping Willow
Hickory	Walnut

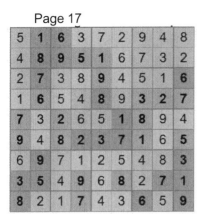

Page 17

5	1	6	3	7	2	9	4	8
4	8	9	5	1	6	7	3	2
2	7	3	8	9	4	5	1	6
1	6	5	4	8	9	3	2	7
7	3	2	6	5	1	8	9	4
9	4	8	2	3	7	1	6	5
6	9	7	1	2	5	4	8	3
3	5	4	9	6	8	2	7	1
8	2	1	7	4	3	6	5	9

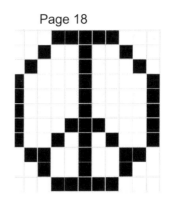

Page 18

Page 19

14

9	4	4	1	18
6	4	3	7	20
8	9	1	5	23
1	6	5	7	19

24	23	13	20	21

Page 20

2	2	2	2	3	3	4
1	1	1	2	3	3	4
1	1	1	3	3	3	4
7	7	8	6	6	5	4
7	7	8	6	5	5	5
8	8	8	10	10	10	11
9	9	9	9	10	10	11

Page 21

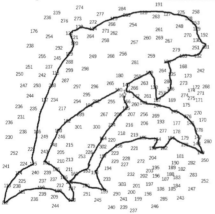

Page 24

Page 22

Hard work doesn't
Guarantee success,
but improves it's chances

Page 25

Page 26

8	-	9	X	2	-10
+	■	X	■	+	
3	X	7	-	4	17
+	■	+	■	X	
6	-	5	X	1	1
17		68		6	

Page 28

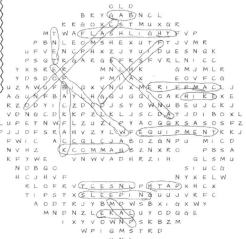

Page 29

Make it your mission to see the good in one person today and tell them.

Page 30

W

Page 31

1	1	1	1	1	5	5	5
9	7	3	3	5	5	5	5
9	7	3	3	3	4	4	4
9	7	7	7	8	8	8	8
9	9	9	9	8	8	8	8
2	6	6	6	11	12	12	10
2	2	6	6	12	12	10	10
2	6	6	6	12	10	10	10

Page 32

4	3	7	9	6	5	1	8	2
6	5	1	3	8	2	4	7	9
2	8	9	4	1	7	6	5	3
7	4	8	2	5	9	3	6	1
9	6	3	1	7	8	2	4	5
1	2	5	6	3	4	7	9	8
8	1	2	7	9	6	5	3	4
3	9	6	5	4	1	8	2	7
5	7	4	8	2	3	9	1	6

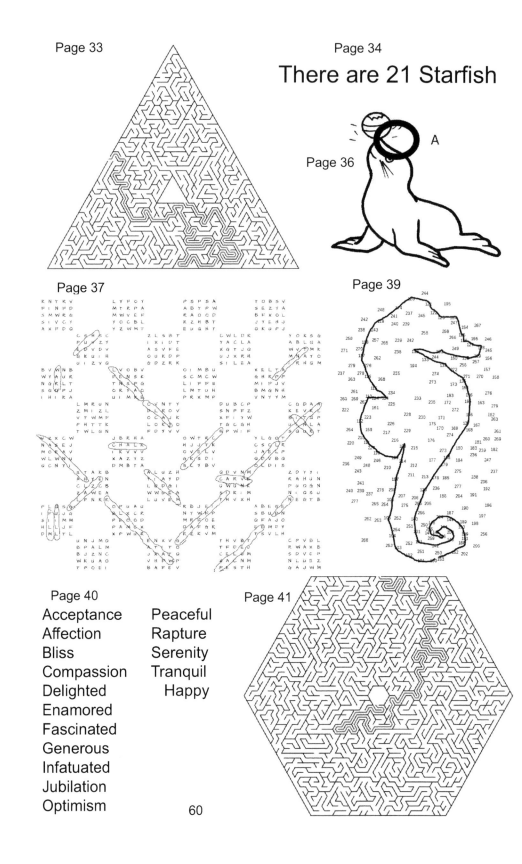

Page 33

Page 34

There are 21 Starfish

Page 36

A

Page 37

Page 39

Page 40

Acceptance   Peaceful
Affection   Rapture
Bliss   Serenity
Compassion   Tranquil
Delighted   Happy
Enamored
Fascinated
Generous
Infatuated
Jubilation
Optimism

Page 41

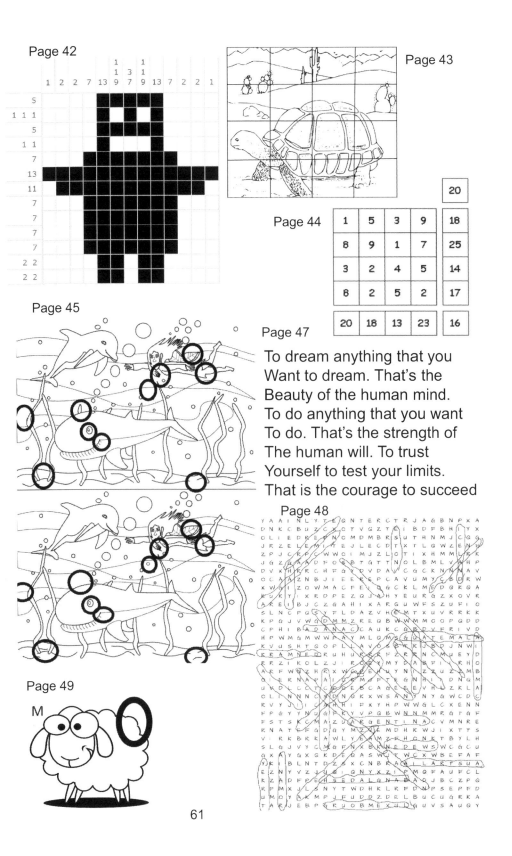

Page 42

Page 43

Page 44

1	5	3	9	18
8	9	1	7	25
3	2	4	5	14
8	2	5	2	17
20	18	13	23	16

20

Page 45

Page 47

To dream anything that you
Want to dream. That's the
Beauty of the human mind.
To do anything that you want
To do. That's the strength of
The human will. To trust
Yourself to test your limits.
That is the courage to succeed

Page 48

Page 49

M

61

People do not realize how close they
Were to success when they gave up.

7	+	6	+	4	17
X	■	X	■	-	
3	X	1	+	9	12
+	■	-	■	-	
8	X	5	-	2	38

29		1		-7

Medium

Life is a very great gift
And a great good, not
Because of what it
gives us, but because
of what it enables
us to give others.

Thanks for your
purchase! Please
leave a review on
Amazon. It is your
greatest complment:)

Books by Tamara L Adams

Mood Tracker Planner
Defiant (YA Dystopian Novel Series)
Art Up This Journal #1 and #2 Series
Backstabbing Bitches: Adult Activities
Puptivities: Adult Activities
Cativities: Adult Activities
Christmas Activities: Adult Activity Book/Bucket List
Activititties: Adult Activities
I Hate My Boss: Adult Activities
Activity Book for Adults
Activity Book You Never Knew You Wanted But Can't Live Without
Activity Book You need to Buy Before You Die
Fuck This Shit: Vulgar Activities
What an Asshole: Vulgar Activities
Fuck I'm Bored #1 and #2 Series : Adult Activity Book
I'm Still Fucking Bored: Adult Activity Book
The Activity Book That Will Transform Your Life
Activities to do while you number two
Unmotivated Coloring Quotes
Angry Coloring
Coloring Happy Quotes
Guided Bullet/Dot Planner
Coloring Cocktails
Cussing Creatures Color
100, 76 and 51 Quote Inspired Journal Prompts Series
Unlocking Happiness Planner
Cleaning and Organizing Planner
Daily Fitness Planner
Bloggers Daily Planner
Bloggers Daily Planner w margins
Writers Daily Planner
Busy Mothers Planner
Where's Woody Coloring Book
99 Writing Prompts
Deciding Destiny Series: Christy, Matt, Joe or Linsday
Rich Stryker Sreies: Julie's Last Hope/Tom's Final Justice
Unlocking Happiness
Getting to Know Yourself Journal and #2 Series
Timmy and the Dragon Children's Picture Book
Jacob and Ronnie the Robot Blast off to the Moon

Check out these other items by the Author:

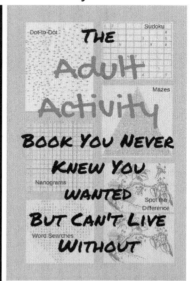

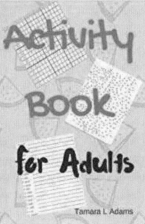

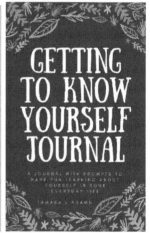

Other
Titles
By
The
Author

Thanks for your purchase!!

Please leave a review! I would be grateful.

Contact me to get a free printable PDF of Activities here at:

http://www.tamaraladamsauthor.com/free-printable-activity-book-pdf/

Tamaraadamsauthor@gmail.com

Thank you for your support and have a great day!

You can contact me at

http://www.amazon.com/T.L.-Adams/e/B00YSROGC4

Tammy@tamaraladamsauthor.com

https://www.pinterest.com/TamaraLAdamsAuthor/

https://twitter.com/TamaraLAdams

https://www.facebook.com/TamaraLAdamsAuthor/

https://www.youtube.com/user/tamaraladams

https://www.instagram.com/tamaraladamsauthor/

http://www.tamaraladamsauthor.com

All Cartoon Drawings are from https://publicdomainvectors.org

Made in the USA
Coppell, TX
22 March 2023

14578224R10039